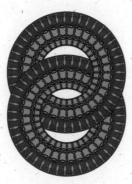

THE DISHEVELED BED

POEMS

THE DISHEVELED BED

POEMS

Andrea Carter Brown

CavanKerry ❖ Press LTD.

Library of Congress Cataloging-in-Publication Data

Brown, Andrea Carter, 1949–

The disheveled bed / Andrea Carter Brown.— 1st ed.

   p. cm.

ISBN 0-9723045-3-3

I. Title.

PS3602.R655D57 2005

811'.6--dc22

                              2004026740

Author photograph by Star Black © 2005

Cover art: "Morning Light, Turkey", oil pastel on panel, 11.5″ x 11″,

by Susan Bennerstrom © 2003

Cover and book design by Peter Cusack

An exerpt from the poem "The Continuous Life," from

THE CONTINUOUS LIFE by Mark Strand, copyright © 1990

by Mark Strand. Used by permission of Alfred A. Knopf,

a division of Random House, Inc.

Two lines from "I Feel Like I'm Fixin' To Die Rag," words and music

by Joe McDonald © 1965, renewed 1993 by Alkatraz Corner Music Co.

Used by permission.

CavanKerry Press Ltd.

Fort Lee, New Jersey

www.cavankerrypress.org

First Edition 2006

Printed in the United States of America

ACKNOWLEDGMENTS

For their support and encouragement, I am grateful to Kim Roberts, Scott Hightower, Megan Sexton, and Etta Worthington. Susan Bennerstrom's beautiful series of paintings of bedrooms are the perfect visual expression of this book; heartfelt thanks to her for allowing one of them to grace its cover. I would also like to thank Joe McDonald for his song, William Belmont for allowing me to quote from it, and Susan Jacobs for her help in finding them. For their love and support over the years, I thank my family and friends, especially my mother, Evelyn Brown, and my sister, Deborah Drake. Lastly, my gratitude to Molly Peacock and the late William Matthews is beyond words.

And to everyone at CavanKerry Press, especially Joan Cusack Handler for her faith in this book and Peter Cusack for his fine eye, a very special thanks.

NEW JERSEY
STATE COUNCIL
ON THE ARTS

CavanKerry Press is grateful for the support it
receives from the New Jersey State Council on the Arts.

Grateful acknowledgment is made to the editors of the following journals and anthologies in which some of these poems, or earlier versions of them, first appeared:

Barnabe Mountain Review: "The Bi-Coastal Body Count Theory of Human Relations"
Borderlands: "Our Lady of Prague"
The Comstock Review: "Fauna peruviana"
The Gettysburg Review: "The Los Angeles at Lankershim" and "Wit's End"
The MacGuffin: "Inside Out"
Many Mountains Moving: "St. Thomas Aquinas and the Brahma Bulls"
The Marlboro Review: "Notes toward an Epistemology of Loss"
Mississippi Review: "45"
The National Poetry Competition Winners: "The Delaware below Merrill Creek"
The North American Review: "The Robin's Nest"
Penumbra: "Point Dume" and "Bonanza"
Phoebe: "The Lopatcong at Swamp Road"
PSA News: "The Life Cycle of a Chicken"
River Oak Review: "The Musconetcong above New Hope"
The Sandhills Review: "Island in the Sky"
The Southern Anthology: "Too Much"
The Wildwood Review: "Brook and Rainbow"

Several of the poems from this collection were published in *Brook & Rainbow*, winner of the 2000 Sow's Ear Press Chapbook Competition and published in April 2001.

"The Life Cycle of a Chicken" won the Gustav Davidson Memorial Award from the Poetry Society of America. "The Musconetcong above New Hope" won the *River Oak Review* Poetry Prize. "Inside Out" won the National Poet Hunt Competition from *The MacGuffin*.

I wish to thank the MacDowell Colony, the Virginia Center for the Creative Arts, and, especially, the Ragdale Foundation for residencies that enabled me to complete many of these poems.

Oh parents, confess
To your little ones the night is a long way off
And your taste for the mundane grows; tell them
Your worship of household chores has barely begun;
Describe the beauty of shovels and rakes, brooms and mops;
Say there will always be cooking and cleaning to do,
That one thing leads to another, which leads to another;
Explain that you live between two great darks, the first
With an ending, the second without one, that the luckiest
Thing is having been born, that you live in a blur
Of hours and days, months and years, and believe
It has meaning, despite the occasional fear
You are slipping away with nothing completed, nothing
To prove you existed.

Mark Strand, *The Continuous Life*

For Tom

CONTENTS

FOREWORD

About ninety years ago Ford Madox Ford seems to have persuaded Ezra Pound that poetry must be "at least as well written as prose." They wanted poets of their day to renounce the sentimental singsong of the previous century and begin to write with the truthful edge and persuasive clarity expected of fiction and essays.

Like Yeats, Andrea Carter Brown accepts that challenge. She writes well by training her intelligence and keen attention on matters of heartfelt importance, and her poems come alive with all the pleasure and pain of living with eyes open.

Most memorably in this collection, Brown records the disappointment and courage of a woman unable to bear the children she and her husband want. Without hedges or illusions, the poems present the crucial details of clinical visits, miscarriage, mourning, and the persistent difficulty of sustaining and reconstructing oneself, one's marriage, and the world.

The Disheveled Bed, in other words, reverberates with the complexities of a whole life, tested by its particular turnings. The poems celebrate the strength of mind and the art that find truths in experience unblurred by evasion.

In one poem the poet tries the difficult pleasure of watching children in the park and remembers her play at their age, until at last she cools her feet in the lily pond and watches herself "stay until I know / my husband will start to worry where I am." This voice of quiet candor, with its intimate trust of the reader, speaks through Brown's poems steadily with confident attention.

In the background of the focal narrative, observations of the textures of city living and visits to the country and the seaside are interwoven with family relationships and the difficult chosen love of married life. When in the title poem the poet hears the songs of the birds under her window, we feel with her: "the random yet orderly / rise and fall of their songs rising as high / as our high-rise home." It's an equally miraculous privilege, as a reader of these vital poems, to find myself in earshot.

Brooks Haxton

Fall 2005

THE DISHEVELED BED

POEMS

Deer Season in Manhattan

It can happen anywhere. And it does
on that crummy corner where Macdougal
crosses 3rd, before the law school tore
down the tenements to build a dorm

named for a chain of supermarkets.
It is after the separation but before
my divorce and her first kid. We
are walking, she with her husband,

I with the man no one can understand
what I am doing with. Where are we
going? Standing on the curb, I catch her
unawares, the down on her smooth cheek

transparent in sun. And the pupil
of her hazel eye, half yellow, half brown,
the shade I used to call baby shit green,
wide open, so I look straight into

her soul, as the poets say, and all
the bad blood between us vanishes,
the festering slights, petty thefts,
lies. For I see now that inside she is

defenseless as Bambi for whom she cried
and cried as a kid. I would give my soul
to save her from what lies ahead, but I
can't. No one can. And this is love.

I

Ultrasound

The alarm crescendos in your ears. Outside
it's still dark. You pee, wipe the sleep

from your eyes, brush hair and teeth,
wash your crotch, drag on yesterday's

slacks and top, walk a block, wake up
the cabbie asleep at the wheel. He likes

your destination. He can take the highway
all the way. It's empty. In the waiting

room next door to the morgue, you join
half a dozen others. Why not have

numbers? You skim the stale *Family
Circles* until your name is called. In

a little cubicle with a draft you strip
from the waist down and wait, a blue sheet

for a skirt, looking at snapshots of babies.
They direct you to a darkened room. You climb

up on a paper-covered table, slide your butt
to its edge, spread your knees. The doctor

enters, slips a regular Ramses over
the probe that vibrates with sound you can't

quite hear, squeezes clear jelly from a tube
onto its quivering tip. She guides it as far

up into you as it will go as her nurse
adjusts the contrast on a tiny television

screen, calls up your history, inserts
the correct date. First they find

your uterus and measure its lining,
piece of cake, but your ovaries play

hard to get. The doctor pushes the stick
this way and that. And you feel

a low-pitched, slippery, beating,
throbbing, barely audible

moan inside you. The right one pops
into view. They count and measure

each black spot, triangulate the depth.
Six 11 x 14 eggs, but the left

ovary eludes her, no, it's right
behind the right. Five here, smaller,

but she's satisfied. She withdraws
the probe, with one motion flips

off the rubber as the last little
black and white pictures develop. "Come

back in three days for another,"
she announces and exits. You return

to your cold clothes, pee, wipe the mess
from your legs, get dressed, write

a check. Outside another five
women wait. You catch a cab, draw

a scalding bath, crawl back into bed.
You dream that you are dead.

(Change of Life on) *Synarel*®

Seven days into it I don't know
myself. Temples tight, lips cracked,
I snap at friends, stiff one cabbie

because he drives too slow, another
for his offer to father himself my child.
Hot flashes, cold waves. Knuckles,

knees give way. Breath, armpits,
feet reek. Teeth ache, nose bleeds
but gums do not, as they should

this time of the month, bloated with
blood that will not come despite cramps
that start and stop. The doctor

promises this will reverse itself
although the drug is so new how can
anyone know? Hair goes limp, falls

out. Making love hurts. I avoid
people, insult my husband. One sniff
in each nostril morning and night,

then waking at 3 a.m. in my sweat-
drenched half of our double bed.
And the terrible thirst.

The Nightgown (Love Poem for a Mother-in-Law)

She was sure I would like it: blue
(her color) flowers on white flannel;
hand-tatting around the neck, wrists,
and hem; and a full skirt and buttons
down the front, should I nurse. I do
like it and wear it three weeks out of
every four when, puffed up with drugs,
my other clothes turn into tourniquets.
Propped up on the sofa then because
my joints are so sore I could weep
but can't take even a single aspirin,
it's re-runs on TV, or re-reading
the mysteries her son gives me each
anniversary (he's inscribed "Here's
Proof with love" on the tenth flyleaf,
the fifth since we started trying) as
hope flows from me until there is none.

IUI (a.k.a. The Double Rainbow)

This cycle the doctor's pleased, meaning
my abdomen's distended to a degree nothing
I can take will relieve, so she's talking

twins and triplets. Or reduction, if necessary,
at nine weeks. The nurse draws my husband's
characteristic pink semen up into a syringe,

eases its curved needle through my cervix
well into my uterus and pushes the plunger,
whispering, "Swim, swim." Suspended

from the ceiling above my head, a mobile
circles slowly in place, turning to a stop
before reversing direction. Red breeds

yellow and blue, which themselves produce
orange and green, purple and ultramarine,
respectively, each reproducing in turn

except the last which, without issue, is larger,
a counterweight to its fertile sibling. My fingers
find the turquoise tadpole strung between turtle

and frog on the fetish necklace I've worn
for luck which you carried home in a sock
to surprise me for my birthday. We saw

our first double rainbow that summer, violets
multiplying in drizzle before our eyes, one
spectrum nestled within another as we do in bed

before sleep. But lying on the examination table
under humming fluorescent tubes in this white,
windowless room, it's hard to believe life

can be made as cramps send out shock waves
through the sheet while I wait out the pain
beneath the rainbow, pleading, "Take, take."

The World Series on *Pergonal*

After you wolf down double-sautéed pork
with chili peppers and I push lemon chicken
over shredded lettuce around the plate, the waiter
brings an orange and two cookies with the check.

Breaking one in half you learn "Patience
will be rewarded," while mine reveals
"You never hesitate to tackle the most

difficult problems" and "A cheerful message
is on its way to you." Eleven innings later

Kirby Puckett hits the blue curtain to tie it up

at three apiece. You're fast asleep on the sofa
as I rock through another night pumped up

with substances banned on the playing field.
Wanting one child, we'll take two, but what
if it's three or more? Every twinge takes on

new meaning: my upset stomach and splitting
headaches, three fortunes in two stale cookies,
our future in the World Series, my Braves
losing on the last pitch to your Twins.

WANTED: RN

Liam climbs up on an over-turned trash basket,
presses his cheeks against the double-glazed pane.
"Truck!" he points and laughs, "Bus!" His mother

and I sneak into her kitchen. Breaking the tips
off four glass vials, she draws sterile solution
into a syringe, drizzles a few drops onto each

of three white pellets which, bubbling, she draws
back up through the bore. With her middle finger
she raps the glass, spritzes the air with *Pergonal*

until the gas inside is expelled. I expose my ass,
turn my toes in, take a deep breath. "Are we left or
right tonight?" We count on fingers to figure which.

A prick. The fluid takes a full fifteen seconds
to invade my muscle: I count. She extracts
the shank, swabs the blood, applies a Big Bird

Band-Aid when it will not stop, and I pull on
my pants just as Liam pokes his head into the room,
his big blue eyes bigger than ever. Since you tore

my number off the flyer I left in the laundry
and offered your help, Nurse Anne Collins
of County Cork, the first girl after seven boys,

with your red hair and green eyes (of course!),
you are better than Cherry Ames whom I worshiped
only in books. And every day when I come to you

15

with my shopping bag of medicine and hope, I bless
you and your handsome chubby son who, after many
months, at last invites me to play with his trucks.

hCG on Christmas Eve (Take 2)

Thirty-six hours later I am afraid
to breathe. 1 a.m. and one hundred
miles from home and doctor, my abdomen
balloons beneath the sheet whose weight is
sufficient to make me scream. My sister
and her four kids sleep, so I grit my teeth

and watch the green eyes of the alarm
watch me. 1:01, :02, :03, :0
four big and six little follicles
pelt the fragile sacks stretched taut
of each over-stimulated ovary
just like those yellow styrofoam

electrons orbiting tenth grade molecules,
though here the negative charges will not
pair up and settle down. "A cycle from
hell," a fellow traveler complains. Is
this what to expect? What if the time
bomb inside me explodes? It's a real

possibility: we've been warned. Two
o'clock. Three. The luminous hours
do pass. At four the dogs next door howl.
By five I can quarter rotate to one side. Six
brings dawn through the drawn blinds,
dimming the radioactive minutes.

I pretend to sleep. That night I'll throw
up everything I've eaten since the shot
on Christmas Eve as my husband, holding

the bucket, mutters, *"Rosemary's Baby."*
And we giggle, can't help laughing
at the idea as I spit up tough stuffed

turkey, giblet gravy, candied yams, creamed
onions, ripe and green olives, and mocha
bundt wreath garnished with glacéed cherries
and citron leaves (because this is how we

always welcome the Christ child), *"Rosemary's*
fucking," we laugh until the bile comes, *"Baby."*

Natural Selection

Two weeks: we're counting. As my beloved
Trollope often wrote, *A fortnight is wanting.*
In almost the time it takes new to wax to full
or full to wane again to nothing, I go through
all the phases from hope to despair. Mother
no doubt prays *Thy will be done*, while my
own doubting Tom, over yet another dinner
delivered from Zen, argues, *It's not over
till the fat lady sings*, whoever she may be.
But in fourteen days, no more. Tomorrow
I may change my mind; today I say no
more shots, stirrups, speculum. Absolutely
no more chemical warfare (Is she or isn't she?)
within me, and after, and despite it all,

no child. I might walk into the ocean
then or we might sail to the islands where
Darwin discovered that finches, isolated
over relatively few generations, evolve
beaks adapted to different needs. And there,
without natural predators, each of thirteen
species in its own niche, the finches live
out their days and die. In a couple weeks,
we may book our berth and set out for
the distant archipelago that sinks even
as it grows from below, before we begin
to build our next nest as best we can, with
what fullness of life remains to be made.

Notes toward an Epistemology of Loss

I

You aren't sure you want one.

II

Watching another couple feed mule deer
Potato chips you decide: Yes.

III

Poor test results but
You test positive.

IV

Before you can tell
It dies. Why?

V

Yes, why not lie
In bed all day?

VI

Trying is antithetical
To desire.

VII

Desire is equivocal;
Still you try.

VIII

Medical knowledge proves
Its ignorance.

IX

Lying on a stranger's bed
ou wonder: Did they? Was she?

X

When you change the sheets you see
Stains older than yours.

XI

What is sleep? You would give
Years for a night.

XII

Come August the flycatchers abandon
The egg that would not hatch.

XIII

You turn toward each other
Because there is no other.

II

The Lopatcong at Swamp Road

Painted daisies. Shasta. Variegated
petunias. Forsythia, *Rachel*, hydrangea.
Phlox, cosmos, poppies, iris, *Elliott*.
Lily-of-the-valley, sweet alyssum,
Aaron, ageratum. Crocus, rose, fox-
glove, daffodil, pansy, portulaca.
Lilac, *Elysia*, bleeding heart, blue
bells, hyacinth, forget-me-not, fuchsia.
Mock orange (syringa), clematis, honey-
suckle, baby tears. So my sister grows
her life. Once in a lifetime I time it
right, and wild violets cover the slope
all the way from her crumbling stone
wall to the creek I follow to my room
beside the river where words come.

My Degas

At the monster show, the kind
so huge they put a rest room
in the back stretch, I am drawn
to the downs, to rolling grass
under overcast skies. A dapper
cabriolet, pulled by a pair
of spirited bays, pulls away
from the course, petite against
the masterpieces which dominate
the gallery, so small in fact it's
easy to mistake its occupants
for a family of three. Of course
it is the man who holds the reins,
a terrier at his side. Behind him,
two women share the seat. One sits
at ease, acres of pale mauve muslin
hogging two-thirds of the space,
forcing her companion, prim
in ruched buttercup silk flounces,
into the far corner. Husband and wife
plus spinster sister or some other
poor relation it would seem, except,
on closer inspection, a breast
pokes through the lavender bodice,
beneath which a minuscule
head rests. What we have
instead is not a racing but
a domestic scene trotted out
into the open: a father, mother,
their baby, and the wet nurse
whose mother's milk nourishes

someone else's child for money.
She steals the show; her flesh
tones warm, against which all
that valuable horseflesh, the rich,
supersaturated fabrics pale.
The man drives his mares,
the mother stares at her child
but does not touch, while the girl,
her full bosom rosy, nestles
the infant with her whole body.

Our Lady of Prague

The eve of her wedding day she prayed
to be saved and woke the next morning
bearded to the waist. The groom
      understandably said *No way*

which was OK by her; but the king,
her father, in a fit of pique, cut
out her tongue, which had cost him
      the bride's price. She bled

blissfully to death a virgin, preferring
martyrdom to marriage with a heathen.
In the crypt, the beard grew
      gray; her body refused

to decompose; then goldsmiths crafted
vessels studded with enormous sapphires
and pearls to house her hacked-up
      miraculous remains. *Kümmerniss*,

trouble raised to a substantive,
they named her at birth, little guessing
how true it would prove, their daughter
      apotheosized to patron saint

of lost causes, fresh-cheeked, whiskers
to her knees, holding court in a corner
chapel of some obscure shrine, where
      the hopeless still seek relief.

The Life Cycle of a Chicken

In soft pencil scratched on a single sheet
of cheap paper, first a fat hen lays an egg,
the big-eyed chick emerges from its shell,
grows up. A woman carries by its legs
a pullet home from the store. Dead center,
an oven. Plucked and roasted, her family
eats the chicken for dinner. The stick figure
daughter, smiling, bears a peep in her belly.
She squats, bare-buttocked, over a bedpan,
excreting a bird. She flings the waste
out a window to the street. It lands
on a garbage heap in an empty landscape,
where even the refuse then vanishes unseen.
Drawn by Madja Rosenzweig, age thirteen,
in 1944 in Terezin.

Fauna peruviana

By dawn the market already
sputters with the give and take
of commerce. Doña Maria stands
erect by the table in her stall.
She wears at least ten
skirts, but no shoes. Strapped
to her breast in a fuchsia
and peacock shawl,
a small brown baby sleeps,
inert in her warmth.
Today she sells a handful
of wild strawberries.
The over-ripe fruit
sprouts mildew dust,
and the red juice of bruised
flesh spreads its stain
on the gray paper where they lie,
a tongue of sweet blood
curled outward on the land.

Madonna and Child

In a cubicle at the IKEA by the airport,
between peeing and wiping I hear
whimpers, a thrump, or possibly
the thrump comes first. From the safety
of my stall I wonder what is going on
out there, then a woman's voice,
exasperated, screeches, "I told you
not to take the lid off. There's
chocolate all down the front
of your new T-shirt." Emerging
from my hiding place, I see a tall
slim blond pushing forty jab
roughly at dark splotches
on a pink Pocahontas jersey
worn by a miniature version
of herself. The daughter
submits to the cold, to the raw
gestures and words. Mothering,
it comes to me that second,
consists partly of having someone
smaller to yell at with relative
impunity. And why not? Why
shouldn't the woman begrudge
the extra hours trying to get out
what won't come out? Where
else will a still clumsy kid learn
that some small heartaches
can be averted? I pull the lever,
two feet of indeterminately gray paper
unroll. I dry my hands, glance
surreptitiously at them. "ERA,"

I want to say, "is good on stains,"
but hold my peace. Perhaps the chocolate
will come out in the wash. Maybe their day
isn't spoiled. Hopefully the daughter
won't hold a grudge against her mother
the rest of her life. Who knows?
We arrive at who we become
by a logic whose mystery
usually eludes us. I leave them
still cleaning up to join my husband.
We order, pack up, drive home, assemble
the double unit called *Akrobat* to house
the clutter we've accumulated
instead of kids.

III

The Last White Christmas

She hesitates then pins her lucky cluster
of silver grapes to a favorite red blazer
which she, a crazy cab ride later, takes off
together with blouse, bra, slacks, and bikinis,

after drinking a quart of water plus a couple
paper cones worth from the cooler till she can
barely breathe for wanting to pee. The technician
spreads cold transparent yellow jelly on her belly,

with his probe takes pictures of the fetus
whose heart beats. "Nothing to worry, although
it *is* small for nine weeks," ringing in her ears,
she dresses so fast the brooch bangs against

the metal table with a hollow note, denting one
grape. Through pinholes in the waiting room ceiling,
Bing and Rosemary cuddle up over *Silver Bells*.
New Year's Eve she loses it, watching Mad Max

slug it out with Tina Turner in the Thunderdome
while her husband, racing to the only drugstore
open that late, pays for the pills that don't work
with the five dollar bill he'd carried years for luck.

Snow falls all night on the pine trees strung
with tiny white lights below their bedroom
window, as the rest of the world pretends
again that this new year will be better.

Inside Out

Thinking to console, one friend,
a father with the usual mixed record,
volunteers *Children are nothing
but heartache*. Another can't help
the non-stop barrage of baby news
only its mother would care to hear.
But *Have you considered adoption?*
takes the cake, that too smooth
conversational segue, as if the two
were interchangeable. If Job had been
a woman she would never believe God
made everything OK by giving another
son or daughter for the one lost, like some
button or broken dinner plate. Good days
I float above it, looking down on my own
little life, the colors alive, the whites
dazzling. On bad, though, stroller gridlock
or a gaggling clutch of new mommies
makes me want to crawl into a hole.
Clichés come to mind: the proverbial rug
pulled out from under you. When Snowcap
was born, we hung his baby picture,
from "The Living Section" of the *Times*,
on the refrigerator door. By the time
we saw him in person, he was three,
almost full-grown, his transparent, hollow
polar bear guard hairs already tinged
aquamarine from chlorine. He swam
constant clockwise circles, rubbing
his forehead against the turquoise
perimeter until it bled. If you scratch a scab

off repeatedly, it leaves a scar. It might
feel uncomfortable, but good, creating
a gap in the thin skin which protects you
from the world, that same membrane
which holds you together, without which
you'd fall apart. Another friend was born
inside out. Her whole life has been one
operation after another, the surgeons
re-inserting organs, restoring
a protective coating. By the time I met her,
she looked just like you or me, with
hands and feet, hair, freckles, a smile,
although she confided she would never
be able to have a child. Scar tissue
is dead; it can't feel or renew itself
like other cells. It just sits there
reminding you of mosquito bites
you scratched until they became infected.
Or the time you wrapped yourself around
a telephone pole. Or let some stranger slit
you open to make you better. Sometimes,
though, a simple prick and the hole
opens up. Then you would give
the world to be once again whole.

The Laparoscopy Rag

What they don't tell you is how much they
don't know, that everything is a crap shoot.

Sure, they can tinker with the trigger, beef
up the "environment," jump start the whole

shebang, open what should be closed, stitch
up the opening that won't hold. They can

ream, steam, and dry clean, as a former lover
was fond of saying in another context; take

still and moving pictures of the hitherto
invisible; slice, dice, dye, count and apply

statistical probabilities. They can kill or cut
out what shouldn't be there; they can make

life in a petri dish, but they can't help you
have a child. And when they're done and

the doctor admits she can't find anything
wrong, she's stumped, *there are some things*

we don't understand, that this is the end
of the road, you're mad as hell. At her,

at the whole fucking rigmarole—furious enough
for Country Joe's song to pop out, *And it's one*

two, three, . . . I don't give a damn, next stop is
but when the madness goes, what's left is . . .

The Ponies (Love Poem for a Father-in-Law)

A carrot-topped toddler teeters toward you,
grabs your arm for support. You let her toy
with your fingers. They are big and strong.
In shade, licking cones after the go-carts,
your wife and son and his wife watch. When

he was this young, you let him eat orange
food until he turned yellow because that was
what he liked. He still loves oranges, apricots
and carrots; I know. Suddenly I'm back at
the inn with mismatched silver and dishes

years ago when we told you our good news.
You smiled as I had never seen before,
from within, and your gray eyes came alive
with ideas: a hand-made cradle, toys. And
ponies, *Would that be OK?*, asking permission

for the first time from your son. Everything
seemed possible then. Now the mother takes
back her treasure, leaving the man who would
have been a wonderful grandfather alone in
sunlight, suddenly old, as we've all become.

Your Dream

A big dog is digging up a hole.
In it lie seven or eight dead puppies.
"My dead babies," you say and wake up.

This morning when you tell me your dream
I cry. "I'm sorry I told you," you repeat,
but I'm not. For the first time, I feel

your grief. Hours later, still in my robe,
I wander to the window. It hardly seems
possible there are people out there going

about their business. The sky is ridged
with the kind of clouds that bring snow.
On the sill, jars full of rocks from

every stream you fished or we hiked
the summer we lived in the shadow
of the Divide. My shaking hands find

the chunk weathered out of the earth
at Animas Forks. Pale as the overcast
heavens that changeable day, its rough

edges smoothed by eons of water rushing
to the sea and as cold as the snowmelt
feeding the stream, I lift it up to

my flushed cheek, hoping it will cool
a too swift heart that wants to burst.

Island in the Sky

Last night in fog a driver hit
a bighorn. We pass the carcass
and the car wreck coming in.
Mist still shrouds the maze
of pinnacles and spires, rolling up
and over the hidden precipice in waves
although the nearest ocean's a mountain
range or two away. We drive straight
to the point and, taking off everything
except socks and sneakers, lie together
on a slab of sandstone blanketed
with orange and sky-blue lichen.
The half-dead pinyon that half
shields us from sun drips
invisible pitch. We stick
to each other and our bed,
prick our skin with needles.
At our feet, the earth drops
a thousand feet to another rim
of rotting stone, and deeper still,
two rivers, one green, the other
mud brown, thread toward each other
for the last goose-necked gasp
through blood-red badlands
and cataracts to the ocean.

Cliff swallows catch the canyon
updrafts just beyond reach. By noon,
the sun, having burned off the fog
and sucked dry the puddles, sends
even the cold-blooded whiptail lizard

to cover. We retreat to a stand
of juniper. In a few thousand years
they've grown just taller than a man,
thick-skinned, male and female
trunks intertwined beneath a canopy
of silver-bearing evergreen.
Huddled there we hear
a hoarse chorus of spadefoot toads.
Since last night's storm, the first
in many months, they've come
out of the earth, lined up
by the dozens at potholes
suddenly lakes. For a few hours
they'll croak their coarse notes,
crooning for a mate until the pool
evaporates and, burying themselves
once again in mud, they await
the next rain's release.

Where do the children go
who die before they're born?
We went to the edge of the world
to make you. And though your heart
beat, we heard it, it stopped
in the last hours of a bad year
we hoped your coming would better.
This New Year's morning, cradling
a mug of milky coffee grown
cold, my heart throbs with
the double blood it no longer
needs. A line of geese
cuts a black diagonal above
the rotten ice floes the wind
blows to my side of this river.
Later, as it did that afternoon

we sat in silence at the world's edge,
out of the west, out
of thin air, the first frail
clouds miraculously appear,
islands in the sky, billowing
and building as they approach
with the dark promise of relief.

The Lily Pond

Sometimes I go where the children play
to pretend, when I feel strong enough,

what might have been and remember
how it felt to splash through puddles

barefoot, or spin in circles until I fell,
shrieking with abandon, knowing

someone watched to make sure
I wasn't hurt. Near the playground,

just down from the merry-go-round,
papyrus, arrowheads, and pure white

water-lilies bloom in the shallow
half-circle where mallards and gadwalls

dabble. Almost invisible in the polished
black granite lip, two poems: I pause

to read. Sometimes I am drawn to "Death
of a Naturalist," but today "The Continuous

Life" makes me stop, slip off my sandals
and dip my toes where the big round lotus

leaves float. The children's din wafts over,
a pair of yellow warblers plunder scraps

of litter for their nest. The cool, clean water
soothes my feet; a sinking sun warms

the backs of my hands. I stay until I know
my husband will start to worry where I am.

Wit's End

Skin on cotton sheets
on polyester padding to protect
the mattress on pine slats
screwed at either end
to the crossbeams between
four posts on woven
wool on rubber on oak
parquet on the poured
concrete floor sunk
on steel pilings to sediments
metamorphosed to gneiss
laid down on bedrock
floating on the Moho
discontinuity,
itself
adrift on magma in which
all elements are said
to reside, so when thought
percolates to the surface,
erupting as sweat, and I throw
off the covers, rotating
on my own axis
clock and counter-clockwise
until, mind drilling
to the center and back
out again winding whole
days up and down
in split-seconds, I must
leave you for iced
mint tea by the window

where almost invisible
tugs illuminated by a single
green globe above each smokestack
ply the smooth black surface
that mirrors stars.

The Disheveled Bed

The birds are back. I like to think
the first two, singing in the pines

four years ago, five floors below,
mated, gave birth, migrated, and came
back with their young, who also bred,

and whose descendants, and theirs,
now pair up and nest, a new generation
every year we've lived here, one extended
and extending family for the one

denied us, the random yet orderly
rise and fall of their songs rising as high
as our high-rise home, as you brush

out my hair and we straighten
together the disheveled bed.

IV

The Art of Transcontinental Commuting

To forestall loss, I take it all
with me: two complete sets of keys;
driver's license, ATM, debit and credit
cards, blank checks, a hundred dollars
cash; distance, reading and sun
glasses; ticket, something to suck
on during take-off and landing, air
sickness pills; laminated instructions
for how to access two answering machines,
voice- and email; address book, stamps
in various denominations; hand lotion,
emery board, comb; travel alarm
with multiple time zones; aspirin
and Advil, Band-Aids in assorted
shapes and sizes; large and small
safety pins and paper clips; a supply
of quarters, nickels, and dimes for pay
phones and toilets; tissues; tampons;
a cigar tin of sharp pencils, one thick
plus two medium paperbacks, a half
full blank notebook and an extra,
just in case; a 3 x 5 card with
addresses and phone numbers
and whom to contact in the event
of an emergency. No matter where
I am then, whether here or there,
even if my luggage is lost, I'll be
OK. I've got what I need.

The Bi-Coastal Body Count Theory
of Human Relations

"Home is where the husband is," I only
    think but you have the guts to say.
We laugh, but it's true. And yet, no matter
    how many meals we cook or how much
love we make in the rooms we now call home,
    no amount of Mr. Clean or Comet
can remove that old Holiday Inn aroma
    or the lethargy we can't seem
to shake. Middle-class migrant workers,
    you follow the work, and I, you.
A winnowing basket from Bogotá; our rocks
    from Cape Cod; my complete Trollope,
Dick Francis, and Rex Stout; pine cones,
    sheets; everything we own I now see
in terms of packing boxes or tag sales.
    Clear away the clutter and a great
emptiness looms, relieved only in part
    by company. I call it the body
count theory: how the proximity of others,
    especially those whose smell
we like, is the only absolute, in
    pursuit of which we put up with
cruelty, cantankerousness, the jockeying
    for power inherent in any
intimacy. And the satisfaction
    of which, however evanescent, is
sufficient to make me give up my life
    in New York just to be unhappy
but with you in LA, so when we both wake
    to the unnatural silence before

the earth and everything on it starts
      shaking, and we can't see anything
clearly, our shaky voices meet across
      the sheets, calling out "Are you
OK?" Later we bury ourselves
      in each other until it fades.

Point Dume

No shells, no skipping stones
like those at home. No eel grass
or seaweed with bubbles we love to pop
but kelp, great mounds like stranded
water moccasin nests, and sand
writhing with fleas. A seal
rolls back and forth in the surf,
bloated, its skull picked
pretty clean. No, it isn't pretty
here; it doesn't even smell
the way we think a beach
should, but late afternoons
we drive an hour to walk a mile
up and back. Once we happened
on a wedding, the graduated
bridesmaids in black velvet;
another time it was a man
suspended from a rainbow
in a sling, who gunned
the gasoline engine at his ass
to catch updrafts. Hours he hung
above the rotting promontory
stabilized by ice plants, showing
off. The gulls ignored him. Back
and forth, up and down, above
the same slight dip in the cliffs
ad nauseam until I'm seasick
and start to worry he's stuck
in a Möbius strip and can't
come down. Will he be able
to manoeuver out over water

before he bails out? Will
invisible currents sweep him up
to the stars? Didn't some god
fall from the sky? Didn't some
hero get stuck in the heavens?
The haze blows away as
it sometimes does this
same hour each day. Against
the sudden blue, the guy
wires shine. Gloved hands
pull to change direction:
his back and forth is a matter
of choice. Being suspended
above the world and between two
lives is neither good nor bad, the way
back and forth and up and down
are not necessarily means
to an end. I wonder what
his life looks like to the man
hanging in the sky. Or does it fall
away from him, up there
with the birds, the noisy
gas guzzler drowning out
every other sound. That must
be peace: feeling nothing
but the breeze on your skin, day
losing its warmth and dusk coming up,
sun and quarter moon inches apart
above a cold, deep ocean, and knowing
you can come and go, in and out
of this and that, at will.

The Los Angeles at Lankershim

After dark when the Santa Anas
    descend from the San Gabriels
to scour out the valley, at midnight
    when almost everyone is
asleep and Saturn with his rings
    shines above our hill, they let

the water out. In silence the river spreads
    to its banks. From resistance
comes sound. A thousand miles it flows
    through aqueducts to reservoirs
that feed the town where succulent leaves,
    jumble of vine, and riot

of weeds exhale moisture back into the air
    each night and released
rainfall resumes its interrupted course
    until morning, when the stream
bed dries up again, save the central trough
    in which, a few feet

wide and one deep, something always flows,
    a black stripe against concrete
containing walls someone spray-painted
    with his initials, R.I.P.,
as what's left of the river descends
    cement steps to the sea.

Bonanza

Dennis Hopper got his big break playing
a preacher's son turned bounty hunter
after Pawnee scalped his ma and pa and
brothers and sister. There was a woman

too, of course, the abused wife the escaped
gunslinger comes for. She goes with him
to save her alcoholic father whom the bad
guy shoots anyway for fun. They hole up

on the Ponderosa until the final shoot-out
when the lawman discovers he cannot pull
the trigger and Little Joe, hiding behind
papier-mâché boulders, kills the killer

and saves Hopper's life. Commercial break.
Time cut. The Cartrights see their new
friend and his new wife off to Bible school,
those scary very blue eyes burning now

with a different light. We watched "Bonanza"
religiously each Sunday night. My sister loved
Hoss best: he was fat and sweet; it hurt him
when he had to hurt others. I liked the whole

above its parts: three brothers and their father
living in relative harmony, their scrapes and scraps
straightened out in an hour, the homestead
that hummed without women, the house that

felt like a home. We should have guessed
then that Dennis Hopper would make, grown up,
a better bad guy. And that Michael Landon
would become a great Pa on his own

"Little House" although for him there would be
no "Happy Golden Years" but a short-lived
"Highway to Heaven." Waiting on line
at the supermarket, I watch him shrivel

week by week as the disease eats him
from within until, the end near, he decides
he wants to be buried beside Lorne Greene,
his *spiritual father*. So he buys

fifty nearby plots for himself and his family,
and is. Dan Blocker went a long time back,
a heart attack, but that Little Joe should go
so young and so bad hits hard. After "Bonanza"

was canceled I stopped believing in life
after death and God. Now I almost wish
I could. Instead, I unpack all the old
dog-eared Laura Ingalls Wilders that once

had saved me and let them again work
their magic as a glossy new life-and-death
story eclipses the last, and some lesser
star makes headlines near the cash register.

At the Public Library

Claudette Colbert as Cleopatra smiles down
from the wall where four times larger than life
she hangs. Below her, a slim Rastafarian thumbs
the unabridged dictionary beside a pockmarked
cowboy who taps his black and white anaconda

boots as he skims *Variety*. Out the big picture
window, above the parking lot, the lush fronds
of palms blowing slow-motion herald the first
rain in months. The sky darkens, beige stucco
walls turn brown, and raptors circle the city

as if it were dead. In here, Bogart and Bergman
say their giant good-byes before she takes off
with Henreid, and he, Claude Rains. Opposite
them, Chaplin promises "six reels of JOY" in
The Kid, although after years of trying, we're

still childless. Birds of prey take what they
and their babies need. At the zoo yesterday,
we paused by a pair sleeping side by side.
If you wait quietly long enough, the animals
will take notice. And, sure enough, the female

(having a less red casque) Javan rhinoceros
hornbill flew down to our corner of their cage.
One by one she picked green grapes up in the tip
of her beak. Tossing back her head as she opened
wide, she caught each grape perfectly until the last

which she carried back to her mate. Beak to beak
they passed the grape back and forth until she, on
his direction, swallowed the fruit. You take me
out to eat every night when I fly out here to be
with you and we try to make a new life.

On the drive up from San Diego, talking
dates and dollars made the move real and I wept
for the family and life left behind, for the children
we lost, and for the other two hornbill couples
we love to visit at the Bronx Zoo, as you steered

us through bumper-to-bumper traffic to that room
with the Murphy, mirror-bottomed, queen-sized bed.
The plants will save me, I hope, the red and purple
bougainvillaea with their papery heart-shaped leaves
blooming improbably now in late fall, and the other

exotics whose names I don't yet know. And above
all, those great birds, soaring overhead wherever
you look. The man with the halo of dreadlocks
has left. In his place, a woman makes herself
at home. In skin-tight, low-cut, lavender

Michael Jackson T-shirt and black mini-skirt,
wearing sneakers missing both toes, it's hard
not to stare at the pencilled-in eyebrows, the Betty
Boop lips and cheeks. And it's impossible to decide
whether she's beautiful, ugly, crazy, or all three,

attracting and repelling as she does at the same time.
Across a table at the public library, her bleached
blond faces my brown turning gray, her false
eyelashes, my wire-rimmed reading glasses.
When she looks up, I look away or down, afraid

to meet in her gaze the cracked mirror image
of my own grief gone wild. At last, having gathered
two armfuls of books, she extracts a dime-store
magnifying glass, snaps the lens into its frame,
and settles. Later, after the front breaks up

without a drop, and a red neon *Hollywood*
gleams from the roof-top, after many others
have also come and gone, we're both still here,
taking consolation from words on the page
as we read and write the hours away.

A Valentine for Miss Van Duyn

Dear Mona Van Duyn (Mrs. Jarvis Thurston),

    You probably don't remember me, but I
have never forgotten the time you confessed
*The pain subsides, but the want never goes away
entirely*. We were sitting across from each other,
rocking on a white porch under tall sweet gums.
Back then, I had just begun, but you had lived
the whole arc: desire, disappointment, despair.
Your words saved me, I know now, helped me
through grief to the beginnings of acceptance,
humor, cheer. Seated in another garden years
later, for the first time I have the guts to read
those *Valentines to the Wide World* in which
you chronicle the loss that laid you low and how
writing brought you back. Surrounded by lilacs
almost too old to flower, a single bird circles.
I don't need binoculars to see it is the rare cross
between Blue- and Golden-winged Warblers:
my first Brewster's. I don't know yet what life
will bring, but I believe, because you wrote it
so, our life will be full, if not with children, then
with other riches. For "Late Loving," especially,
for "A Reading of Rex Stout," and for "Goya's
'Two Old People Eating Soup'," for "Letters
from a Father," "The Block," and for "Caring
for Surfaces," I thank you from the very bottom
of my mending heart.   Yours most sincerely,

Andrea Carter Brown (Mrs. Thomas Drescher)

V

Neither Here Nor There

Versatility is one of your outstanding traits.
You are the master of every situation.
—two fortunes in one cookie

I

Tuesday: The First Night Back in New York

Walking up and down our bowling alley
living room: over-stuffed, floor to ceiling
books, dust collectors, memories, gloom.
I broil a steak, steam green beans,

feel for the glass knob on my great
aunt's washstand and pull out a napkin
without thinking. This is what *home*
means. Is *this* what home means? In

high-rises across the street, I can see
into other people's lives. I masticate
the tough meat, squeaky beans. Give
me a week and the worst will pass,

two and I'll be OK, but tonight I crave
the light that sucks everything bone dry,
peaks invisible in haze until day fades.

.

II

The Morning After: Wednesday

Turning off the alarm I'm surprised to see
I've dozed through everything from weed
whacker to recycling truck, the hydraulic
groans and squeals alternating with cracks
as glass shatters in its hold. On the toilet
I wonder what happened to the bath towel
missing from the rack. Then last night
slowly comes back: unsatisfying straight-
to-video thriller followed by box-office-flop
tear-jerker. Too wired to sleep, skimmed
a book I thought would be better. Several
trips to the kitchen for stale, unsalted
pretzels. On the bedstand, crumbs.
Below, on the floor, the missing towel.

How in the world did *that* get *there?*
Dimly I remember waking terrified
someone would break in and going
out wrapped in a towel to bring my bag
near me, as if that would keep us safe.
Did I sleep at all? The day is muggy
and overcast as I had forgotten it
often is back east. How will I fool
myself into sleep tonight? As long
as my body stays in your time zone,
eating dinner at midnight, not rising
until noon after falling off near dawn,
I can pretend we're not a continent
apart. I think I'll rent three movies tonight.

III

Thursday: The Next Day

The phone rings twice. Mother-in-law,
then oldest friend—I put off both. Out
the window, the Viking Princess cruises
into port. I consider the waters. How
quickly should I plunge back in? Same
old horizon, threatening sky. Stacks
of catalogues, out-of-date magazines.
I should unpack. The prospect of
a gray day gives me that sinking
feeling. Fill the hours or free-float?
Fresh coffee, I need that. Shall I rouse
myself? Get dressed? I've been months
without rain. If it does, I'll go out.

IV

In-Between: Saturday

German has the perfect word
for this: *inzwischen*. Its middle
swish and the almost impossible
for us to pronounce proximity of
z, *w*, *s*, and *c* strike me today as
infinitely superior to our own
in-between. Taking the English
apart, though, we do get existence
preceded by the prefix for toward
and followed by, I'll speculate,
a variation on *twain*, which over
centuries we've reduced to *two*.
My ancestors came from Stuttgart
and Scotland; my husband works
half the time in LA; I divide mine
between here and there. We talk
on the phone every day, sometimes
twice. What do we have but words?

V

Sunday: No Rest

A lifetime ago, it seems, I first read
and hated *These Twain*. Why should love
succumb to centrifugal force? But you put
something in motion and there's no telling
where it will go. Passion, familiarity,
boredom, indifference, anger. We prize
faithfulness because it is rare. Why am I
here if you are there? Our words ricochet off
man-made planets orbiting the earth. After
fifty years together, my parents are talking
divorce. Each day apart you become less
real. I love reading in bed as long as I like.
I run myself ragged. This is the life.

VI

Thursday, Again

10 days since we said good-bye, 2 weeks
without *it*, I wake up humping the bed. If
you were here, I'd pretend it didn't happen,
hoping you hadn't noticed. Or, if you had,
we might laugh and I might concoct some
story to satisfy your desire to satisfy me.
Such small deceits seem sometimes necessary.
As it is, I won't have to skulk around all day
bashful and ashamed. And secretly proud.
I can let my loose limbs sink into sleep,
hoping they find their way back to the place
mind and body become one and no questions
go unanswered because everything goes.

VII

The 11th Day: Friday

Prime. Indivisible
by anything except itself
and one. True. In the news,
word problems I used to be able
to solve. So much goes. In German
"failure" translates *fallen through*.
My life spins like a worn-out probe
that's missed its goal. My oldest niece
just left for college. So much comes back.
This fall her mother and I will try to find
a nursing home for our parents. "Who will tell
us we need to take a bath when we are old?"
you ask. I want to be the kind of couple
who don't survive each other by much,
the kind of widow who dies soon
after her husband. Forty-seven,
fifty-nine, seventy-one, all
prime, eighty-three or -nine
would be nice as long as we
both can talk and walk and
want to hold each other.
The rest won't count.

VIII

Another Sunday: The Next to Last Day Apart

I think a lot about *penultimate*. Stripping
it down, the logic shines through, but as
a word, it just doesn't cut the mustard. Even
knowing the value of vitamins I have trouble
feeding myself properly. It's pizza-to-go,
order-in Chinese, or scrambled eggs every

night this week: sick food until I'm sick
of that too and borderline sick from lack
of sleep coupled with an absence of leafy greens.
On a whim, I meet my best friend at Anglers
and Writers and, suddenly starved, go whole

hog from vichyssoise through leg of lamb
with mashed potatoes to chocolate layer cake
better than my mother ever made. We've known
each other all our adult lives. These days

we don't know where *we're* going, whether
our friendship will survive. Instead we talk
tying flies, antique bobs and floats, her

dead mother's recipe for shortbread until
we close down the joint, which helps.

IX

The Last Day: Monday

1. Noon

You call me at the office. "There's not enough
room for all your clothes." This is the last
thing I need right now. "I want the black and
white pants for hiking." "What about these
knee socks?" Last winter seems like eons ago.
I wrack my brain to remember what you have
of mine, what fall in the San Juans will mean.
"Rain slickers: we'll need them." "Tell me
what to send." I keep telling you what to bring.
By the time we're done, neither of us is sure
of anything. "Will this be our last conversation
before meeting?" you ask. "I'll be up late;
call when you get home from the beach. Say
hello to the Pacific for me," meaning good-bye.

2. Midnight

Thirteen days since I left you; one
more before I leave to be with you
again. Time to stop the *Times*, clean
out the fridge, hold the mail. By now
I could almost do it in my sleep.
Deciding what to take I feel a little
like God deciding who shall be saved.
As I sort and fold, the apartment
takes on a life of its own. I turn on
all the lights, slam doors, rattle

drawers, hum along with Emmylou.
It's no use. The last leftovers for supper,
my bags locked and lined up by the door.
How ever will I get through the night?

X

Tuesday Yet Again, or *2 + 13 = 14 + 1*

The state where we will meet boasts more
than fifteen fourteeners strung along the twisted
Divide like a strand of freshwater pearls
abandoned during love-making. We last came

to this valley two years ago to leave behind
what we couldn't change. The highest we made it
then was 12,000 feet. At Quartz Ridge the world
fell away but I wouldn't let go. Crisscrossing

the continent has since become a way of life.
This time when my heart beats as if it might
break, I know it won't. Far below, the frosted
Front Range beckons. From opposite directions

our planes approach; somewhere in the terminal
we'll find each other before the next flight.

VI

The Black Canyon

Skirting the Divide they took the Million
Dollar Highway up and down the mountain
stained red. That night she felt weak. By dawn
she was sick as a dog (though not with the morning
sickness she so long had sought). So they did

the drive-through thing, skipping willy-nilly
half the scenic overlooks, peering at some of
the oldest rocks on the planet without binoculars
or bothering to learn their names. They might as well
not have come. Heading back, to perk her up

he pulled in at every fruit stand until they found
"the one." Raspberries, honey, jalapeños; beefsteak
tomatoes, fat runner beans; butter-and-sugar corn;
muskmelons, watermelons, plums. And apricots,
some petite as the nail on your pinkie. "Babies,"

he called them, popping three into her mouth whole.
Bags filled up the back seat, the trunk, more food
than two alone could ever eat; still they kept coming
back for a glimpse of the baby napping in the shade
of the register who was not, alas, they asked, albeit

with a laugh, for sale. With regret they left then,
climbed the same rusty mountain and descended to
the dark house that caught the sun a scant hour each
day before Blue Mountain blocked the light. They
ate as much as they could, but most of it spoiled.

San Juan de los Caballeros, after Ansel Adams

Down the dirt road at the *Rio del Oso*,
three beefy brown men with rice-and-bean
physiques stop work on an antique backhoe

to give us the evil eye as we drive past,
double back, and park. Outside the sanctuary,
enclosed by freshly white-washed railings,

Lorenzo, Pantelion, and José, three brothers
who died within days of each other on the march
to Bataan, lie feet facing the double doors

painted sky blue to ward off the devil. I wade
through hip-high weeds teeming with cicadas
to read the writing on their stones. Someone

has planted and watered and fed and trimmed
sweet bluegrass above the remains. Out back,
by the other graves, carrion-fat crows

line the barbed-wire fence where a large
hand-lettered sign warns photographers
not to steal the souls. Here pink and blue

and red and yellow plastic rose hearts
spell love in all weather: *Husband, Son,
Dad.* Who will come when we are dead?

Late afternoon thunderheads gather across
the same flood plain. Another waning moon
rises above the worn-down peaks. Rootless,

without children or belief, where will we
find peace? Back in the rented house,
for weeks we fall asleep holding

each other and wake the next morning
still intertwined. Summer winds to a close.
The water-greedy cottonwoods, good

for nothing but shade, lose their green
while a rainbow multiplies its blues
before our eyes and two days solid rain

re-covers the distant Divide with white as
we prepare to leave with no answers in sight.

St. Thomas Aquinas and the Brahma Bulls

After the cowgirls' cloverleaf competition,
the elk-calling contest, and a family of four
jumps in and out of a spinning rope circle
to "God Bless America," a man in a pink
and purple satin shirt and chaps leads six
white bulls with dinner plates growing
straight up between their shoulders into
the ring. Nose to tail they trot two by two
around him, then, *wonder of wonders*, three
abreast, followed quickly by the *pièce
de résistance*: with whip and prod and God
only knows what else, he coaxes these bulls
up onto stools no larger than their hooves
where they teeter as he bows to the ground.

The first time I saw "La Conquistadora"
she wore black and that fish-eye expression
mothers have meaning *you can do no right*.
While others lit candles and prayed, I told her
off and went my way. But faith requires
only need. Those who seek, the book says,
shall find. After the rodeo I find myself
again before her, that forbidding gaze grown
five years later more fitting. *May bitterness
not poison my heart.* (The plea of all vanquished
is good enough for me.) Some may care how many
angels can dance on the head of a pin; give
me St. Francis any day, his bare feet planted
on earth, his punctured palms lifted in submission.

Animas Forks

What is it with ghost towns? We follow
the *River of Souls* as close as we can get
to its source, our aging Accord straining
up the gorge, beyond blacktop, past gravel
and rutted mud to hardpan which scrapes

the exhaust system, about which we bicker
for months, each blaming the other. And in
that fine mist each summer afternoon brings,
we park by the outhouse that marks the edge
of the town and head for the only house left

with three stories and a picture window
which rumor has it was built by the "Gold King"
before he struck it even richer at Camp Bird
on the other side of Red Mountain and gave
an opera house to Ouray. It's hard

to imagine how these shacks survived
avalanches, or how anyone can do anything
just shy of twelve thousand feet. They say
people living in the high Andes have hearts
twice as large as ours: we're walking slow

motion just to keep from throwing up.
By mid-summer the blues are already on
their last legs, but pearly everlasting
thrives and wild strawberries ripen to
cultivated proportions. In its heyday,

women came, planting tomatoes and painting
columbines on dinner plates mail ordered
from Syracuse, New York. Their children
went to school here, and the town boasted
two jails, a telegraph and telephone, three

newspapers each week and two hundred
souls. Ten years or so it lasted, until the silver
standard was abandoned and everyone moved
further west. Lichens do well here,
flowering over the raw rock in blotches

of chartreuse, orange, and sage. Lying
on them, hanging over the point of the Y
where the clear east branch of the Animas
falls into the lime-opaque west, I grasp
the salt-and-pepper speckled specimens

you extract from its bed until we can agree
on the perfect one to keep. Flat on my stomach
there, protected from the blast that rushes
down Treasure Mountain, the ruched perimeter
of fungus married to algae tickling my cheek,

for a split-second I understand why we come
to where water decides to flow to one ocean
or the other. Not far above us, the Divide beckons,
less majestic than scruffy. We could clamber up,
but don't. Don't we already know the heartache

of belonging nowhere? Nearby, a family of four
prospects in the tailings for diamonds and rubies
in the rough. In the dust we see a rock with a hole
through its center framed by crystals, the needled
window on emptiness we decide to carry home.

Brook and Rainbow

"Go ahead, touch," you said so I petted
both almost dead fish. A drool of blood
clung to the rainbow's underslung jaw.
By default I know the brook, its flanks
delicately freckled, tawny as a smog-bound
sunrise. A scant hour later and I can't
believe the change: the rainbow's pastel prism
purpled over; the brook's spots swollen
into splotches, enormous empty fish-eyes
staring back. I watch you scale, slit, gut,
wash, dry, dust with salt and peppered flour,
pan-fry and filet them. On my plate, two

half fishes: you won't tell me which is
which but it's plain to see each carries
into death something of life—pink, blue,
and green veined near-translucency beside
opaque late summer sunset. We take a bite
of brook, one of rainbow. Then another
rainbow, and a brook, until tiny bones
fringe the rim like lashes. Why should we
have to choose? Yet, even when we don't,
we do. If I could, would I undo everything
we've been through? Any scientist knows
a rainbow doesn't actually exist, except

in the mind's eye. Just try to hold on
to flowing water, it escapes or becomes
something else. But one changeable day,
showers vying with sun, you brought us
both, brook and rainbow, and I wouldn't

trade the heartache that brought us to this
happiness for the world. If I had to,
I guess I'd take the brook, its down
to earth sweetness, the miracle of bugs
converted to tender muscle, like love
fattened on grief, lingering sweeter
on the tongue for what it's consumed.

Transubstantiation at Creede

Fourteen and a half inches: the biggest
since one escaped through a tear in the net
his dad lent him when he was ten. Fifteen,
maybe, still one shy of the legal minimum

for this stretch of the Rio Grande. Cooing
to soothe the muscled glitter that wriggles
as he tries to slip the hook from its lip,
the fisherman wrestles with his conscience:

to cheat or release. Out of sight around a bend
upstream, his wife studies the undersides
of purple flowers, trying, once again
without success, to figure out the difference

between sticky aster, daisy and fleabane.
Increasingly, at forty-three, she thinks
about the past. Most of us can count on
one hand the times that changed forever

the trajectory of our lives. The son has
yet to forgive his father that long ago hole;
the daughter finally decides to wear the wine
dress given by the mother whose touch she

no longer hates. It *is* better to tame than slay.
Out of water, the rainbow quickly fades. Her
husband cuts the transparent leader, lowers
his catch into the stream. Stunned, the trout

rests a moment on his palm, then shuddering,
revives, rushing back to obscurity, his favorite
Black Fury, the last from True Value, the lucky
lure, disappearing into the depths of the pool.

The Musconetcong above New Hope

At three he rose, by four he was
on the road, driving the used mint
green Fury those last fifty odd miles

he first drove east after the war,
the first of his family to leave.
46 dead ends at Lake Hopatcong;

then it's local roads winding down
Schooley's Mountain to Hackettstown
Diner and left along the stream that,

swelling as it drains, spills into
the river where, trapped under a raft,
he first learned fear. Norm and Bill

and Furm and Jack wade in, fan out,
stake their pools. Their creels soon
fill with brookies, browns, and a rare

rainbow while Andy loses spinners,
nightcrawlers, and his balance before,
at long last, he gets hit. A bottom

heavy, not much fight, ugly
anus-mouthed sucker whose eyes
could kill. He cuts the line

rather than touch it. Hours pass
without another nibble. His right big
toe, frost-bitten after V-E Day,

throbs in the cold, but his buddies
aren't ready to go, one perfect foot
long trout after another rising

to their flies until each has caught
his legal limit and then some. For lunch
it's leftover meat loaf on Wonder Bread

oozing with ketchup, Pabst
Blue Ribbon and black coffee before
the ride home. Late afternoon he pulls

in. And spreading yesterday's *World
Telegram and Sun* on the grass out back,
he takes Norm or Bill or Furm or Jack's

extra trout and slits its belly. The blue
blood and guts spill over the same small
square hands that every Sunday night soaked

the cast off his daughter's leg because she was
afraid of the saw. Then he might tell her
about the sucker and his little luck.

The Delaware below Merrill Creek

Early evening in late May and Hope is
trouncing Harmony with two down
in the bottom of the fifth. Mist intensifies
to drizzle as the shortstop steps to the plate.
Five throws and the count's full. His coach

calls time, whispers instructions. Back in
the box, the batter scuffs the chalk lines,
steps out to practice his swing as the pitcher
winds up to throw. The wet diamond glows
emerald green. Behind home, across the fertile

flood plain, the Water Gap gapes, while beyond
center field, Scott Mountain grows a brilliant
double rainbow. In pipes buried beneath the grass
at our feet, the Delaware flows up to the lake
made to cool down the nuclear power plant

at Upper Black Eddy. Beneath the purple, we can
just see one of the reinforced concrete dikes
covered with gravel where nothing is allowed
to grow except rows of razor wire which surround
the stocked trout swimming above submerged houses.

And halfway between the reservoir and the river
it drains, in the park built to placate the towns-
people living below, boys and girls in uniforms
donated by the power company play in the rich
supersaturated light. The little shortstop at last

manages a single through the gap, but he's thrown
out sliding into second as the heavens open up,
drowning both rainbows. Then the game is
called, though too late for him. The rest of us
look up and hope the containing walls hold.

Hearts

Playing hearts with my parents,
It's not as though I crippled you
Mother hazards as she laughs,
her Queen of Spades, thirteen points
against, she's laid on my club deuce.

The witch, my father chuckles,
Old maid, he looks me in the eye,
butt of easy jokes, single woman
I still seem to be, with a husband
but no child at my side.

Though I take the other
hearts, I cannot help but lose
for my mother holds the tiny two
I dumped on her diamond ace
first time she lead the suit.

When all the tricks are played,
we count to see who's won.
With the Queen of Spades and all
the hearts but hers I'm down,
twenty-five to one.

Father tallies the score.
Husband shuffles the deck.
Mother cuts the pack. I deal
clockwise around the square
four hands of thirteen each.

The game begins again.

Milk

Raw end of winter. Mist on the verge
of congealing. In a pasture six pure white
cows, their three calves, and one Black
Angus chew a path through the swath
of straw a farmer spread. The ruminant
stomach is even more complicated
than the human, which is why we get
sick on grass whereas these cows
ignore the apple I toss over the fence
in favor of hay. Eight hours a day
they ruminate, that is to say, they
chew balls of regurgitated grass,
swallowing, then coughing up
the same mouthful over and over
until, the tough leaves and stems
broken down, the cud passes on into
and through the third and fourth, *true*,
stomachs. What a life.

                    I've never tasted
milk straight out of a cow. The stuff
I pour over cereal comes from a plant
in an industrial park where, first,
by law, they heat it up to kill off
anything that grows, then, by choice,
force it through an orifice to break down
the fat globules small enough to be
suspended. There was a time milk arrived
on the doorstep in glass bottles capped
with waxed paper. There were two kinds
of kids then, those who loved the skin

floating under the lid and the rest
of us who wouldn't touch the stuff
until some grown-up skimmed it off
or shook it in. The two new breasts
I once tried to hide under T-shirts, I know
now, will never nurse. No piercing cry
in the middle of the night will release
streams of sticky colostrum my husband,
out of curiosity as much as love, will want
to taste. Then again, my own mother
didn't nurse. Back then we still embraced
Progress; a whole generation drank
cows' milk through sterilized rubber nipples.
And believed it was better. Every year
from now on, my breasts will be pressed
in a vise until they ache, shot through
with rays to check for growths.
If I'm lucky I won't lose one
or both before I die.

                    The youngest
calf, still bright white, nuzzles up
to his mother's udder. She stands
stock-still for him, her jaws moving
as regularly as my heart, errant
strands of straw protruding from
her muzzle. I finger my chin
for the two hairs sprouted there
recently. It's a losing battle but, what
the hey, lest your bones disintegrate,
don't forget that quart of milk a day!

Living on *Advil* with Ross Macdonald and Rex Stout

They say it's different for everyone
and then they say wildly divergent
levels of pain are common. Basically

they don't know but won't say they
don't know. We do know my womb
has grown a grapefruit-sized tumor,

a fibroid, which they say is common
in women my age. I'm lying on the same
sofa where I lost our child. Since then,

the rose jacquard fabric has cracked
to blotchy rust, but the new orange plush
cozy on the hot water bottle from Dublin

holds and distributes its heat well.
I finish *The Moving Target*, move on
to *The Chill*, re-reading the mysteries

at random this time, grabbing which-
ever volume from the pile on the floor
my hand finds. The dark sky loses

its blackened blues; the world turns
gray before dirty white. My eyes
drift shut; back in bed I snuggle

up against my husband's warm butt.
In half an hour his alarm will go off.
Only four more little red pills allowed

until the next middle of the night. When
I'm through with Lew Archer, there's
still all thirty-nine Archie Goodwins.

The Wedding Dance, after Brueghel

The bride wears black, and russet locks
cascade down her back, the only female
whose hair isn't under wraps. She looks
bemused, as if she already knows a thing
or two. Her scrawny mate, these things
being relative, looks to the heavens. No
spring chicken, has she wed the village
idiot or, worse, dreamer to avoid being
an old maid? It's clear she will keep
a roof over their heads although whether
any chicks come remains, they would say,
the will of Him. Down in the corner,
a pot-bellied man in crimson coaxes
a plaintive gigue out of his inflated gut.

Just as before when on "doctor's orders"
they tried the Atlantic Double Dunes,
Holiday Inns, and the Maid of the Mist,
they lay in makings for carbonara, chill
an extravagant chardonnay and, when
their bed's been set, strip. Then he inserts
North by Northwest into the slot, and they
dig into the communal bowl in technicolor
dark. It was fun as long as they believed
it would work. Life often seems empty
now: the work alternating with amusement
without purpose, the two of them out of sync
with the world. Dinner in bed with Hitchcock
still helps though these days they do it to forget.

Macy's *Memorial Day Mattress Extravaganza*

By the time we give up, double is no longer
enough, so we take the subway to 34th Street.
As sales clerks and other customers watch
we cuddle up on the floor samples. They blush,
but we are having fun. To top it off you run
into an old girlfriend. Queen versus King,
each of us carries the weight of the child

who was not to be: we need more room
just to turn on our nocturnal spits without
waking the other; so we can make love
without falling to the floor. We change
what we can. By throwing out the old bed
we set forth on our new life, though it takes
much longer before we sleep through the night.

The Robin's Nest

My last morning in your home,
after you leave for work, I do
the usual things: drink more coffee
than I should, wander through
each room, pausing to look out
every window, walk your 3½ acres
one last time, for the first time

taking pictures. The jack-o'-lantern
by the front door, his toothy grin
slumped into a grimace. Two stones
you've moved from home to home.
Mother's irises, Aunt Ethel's lilies-
of-the-valley, a cutting off Dad's
pink fairy rose bush, the clump

of forget-me-nots a friend promised
to tend until you put down roots
again. Thirty-six exposures go quickly.
With none left and nothing left to do
but leave, I ease my bare hand
into the female holly, extract
last spring's nest. Inside, a scrap

of sky, robin's egg blue: this nest
was used. Your first two have fledged
and flown; your last two will have to
from another home. Now neither of us
knows where she will live. Too delicate
for human hands, the unkempt cup
disintegrates on touch. I am afraid

to move. In the grass, an abandoned
turquoise frisbee. Perfect, I think,
hoping the kids won't miss it. The nest
in a nest on the seat beside me, I ease
my aging Accord through the gap
in the crumbling stone wall, turn left
onto Swamp Road and don't look back.

Too Much

The slightest hint we're here and the ducks
                    disappear, the loch rising
to the sky in waves, the whoosh of wings

drowning out the winter's wind. A single
                    pair of pochards, almost
invisible, stick to their rock. Skirting

herds, we hug the shore, scare a couple
                    snipe into zigzagged flight,
and, hiding behind a hawthorn blind, spy

a line of cow-licked lapwings, their sleek
                    black and white plumage
emerald in sun. By mid-afternoon nightfall

you're sick as a dog from the reduced cream
                    lake on which the chef floats
every course. By dawn I'm holding cold

towels to your delirious brow, begging you
                    not to die as your dead weight
twitches in my arms; you choke on your own

tongue. Without children, we never had
                    to learn how to take care
of others, which symptoms mean food

poisoning, plain old-fashioned flu,
                    and worse, what to do
for each. In wooziness you drift

away from me. I can't think of anything
       to keep you awake except
naming the presidents, which you reel off

slow motion but correctly until the country
       doctor with aquamarine
eyes pronounces you'll live, it's safe

to let you sleep. I let you, then, my heart
       racing, and go to the solitary
secretive water rail who returns to the reed

beds below our window just after sunrise
       every morning, foraging
where the river empties itself into the lake

without fear, without knowing we are here.

45

Some nights I look up to see the sky
unnaturally mauve. Is this *twilight*
or *dusk*? I look it up. According to
Funk & Wagnalls, the difference lies
in the degree of brightness. The sun
having set, it's not night yet: this

then is twilight. For a change
the dictionary proves sufficiently
specific to be useful; so often
definitions bounce from hay rick
to stack and back, from diligence to
victoria to cabriolet without giving

a clue what each is. We may be
the last generation able to read
Roman numerals. Does anyone else
remember alternating male and female
hurricane seasons? We mispronounce
gigabyte (with a hard *g*); how long

before its origins are lost? A little boy
looks at a rotary phone and wonders
how it works. Did anyone ever
catch tears with a tear-catcher?
As for love, we all know how
little that lasts. Gloaming, now

that's a word. Besides the numinous
lavender, what do we have? Velvet black
trees, a breeze sweeping the day clean.

NOTES

Section I: The medical terms in this section refer to medicines and procedures common to the treatment of infertility. During the process described here, a woman's normal hormonal cycle is suppressed by drugs (in this case *Synarel*) in order to induce a reproductive cycle under more medically controlled conditions. During this phase, *Pergonal* is injected daily to stimulate the production of eggs (follicles) and a richly primed uterus; a shot of hCG then triggers the ovaries to release the eggs. At this point, sperm is collected under lab conditions, washed to enhance its mobility, and injected into the womb by a catheter threaded through the cervix; this last procedure is referred to as IUI, or intrauterine insemination. The whole process is accompanied throughout by frequent blood tests and ultrasounds and has usually been preceded by extensive but largely noninvasive procedures and drugs such as *Clomid*. Each treatment cycle requires at least three months and can be repeated a number of times.

"The Laparoscopy Rag": The quote at the end of the poem comes from the refrain of "I Feel Like I'm Fixin' To Die Rag" by Country Joe and the Fish, one of the classic anti-war songs of the Vietnam era.

"San Juan de los Caballeros, after Ansel Adams": The pilgrimage that this poem describes was prompted by Ansel Adams's 1941 photograph titled "Moonrise, Hernandez." A high percentage of soldiers from New Mexico served in the Philippines during World War II, so it is not as unlikely as it would seem that three brothers died on the Bataan Death March in April 1942.

"St. Thomas Aquinas and the Brahma Bulls": "La Conquistadora" is the oldest continually venerated Madonna in the United States. Brought to Sante Fe, New Mexico, almost 400 years ago, she stands today in the north transept chapel of the cathedral of St. Francis Assisi.

"45": This poem is dedicated to the memory of William Matthews.